FACT FRENZY

REPTILE FACT FRENZY!

by Arnold Ringstad

CAPSTONE PRESS
a capstone imprint

Published by Capstone Press, an imprint of Capstone
1710 Roe Crest Drive, North Mankato, Minnesota 56003
capstonepub.com

Reptile Fact Frenzy! was originally published as *Totally Amazing Facts About Reptiles*, copyright 2018 by Capstone Press.

Library of Congress Cataloging-in-Publication Data
is available on the Library of Congress website.

ISBN: 9798875254802 (hardcover)
ISBN: 9798875254758 (paperback)
ISBN: 9798875254765 (ebook PDF)

Summary: There's a REPTILE FACT FRENZY headed your way! Did you know that a blindfolded pit viper can still catch its prey? Or that a leatherback sea turtle can make a sound like a human burp? Whether kids are in the mood for a quick look or an absorbing read, they're sure to learn some fascinating reptile facts as they scurry through these pages.

Editorial Credits
Designer: Jaime Willems; Media Researcher: Svetlana Zhurkin; Production Specialist: Whitney Schaefer

Image Credits
Getty Images: Alphotographic, 61 (bottom), by wildestanimal, 41 (sea turtle), Cede Prudente, 22, Jason Edwards, 31 (middle), Julian Gunther, 45, Jupiterimages, 54, kozorog, 51 (bottom), McDonald Wildlife Photography Inc., 37 (middle), 53, Peter Finch, 55, Ted Mead, 48, witte-art_de, 59; Shutterstock: Aaron of L.A. Photography, 25 (top), AlexanderTrou, 35 (football field), Aliaksandr Radzko, 3, 7 (top), 17 (bottom), 25 (bottom), Aman Rochman, 63, Andrey Gudkov, 47, Anita Kainrath, 36 (top), Anton MirMar, 52 (bottom), archivector, 39 (rocket), asawinimages, cover (top left), Baishev, 26 (middle right), Birute Vijeikiene, 30 (bottom), Black Creator 24, 31 (top), Brent Coulter, 9, Carboxylase, 29 (tears), Catchlight Lens, 46 (top), Cathy Keifer, 60 (middle), Chantelle Bosch, 23 (top), chriscasey, 49 (top), CkyBe (speech bubble), 5 and throughout, Clint Lockwood, 23 (bottom), Colomba Rossa, cover and back cover (lizard background), DSlight_photography, 19, dwi putra stock, 16 (top), 40 (middle), EcoPrint, 24 (bottom), 28 (top), Edwin Butter, 15, Eric Isselee, cover (top right), 1 (bottom), 5 (bottom right), 21 (snake), 35 (middle), 46 (bottom), 49 (bottom), 64, Eugene Troskie, 16 (bottom), Fiona M. Donnelly, 8, fivespots, 33 (turtle), Folkmother, 44, FotoRequest, 28 (bottom), G. D. Lohar, 24 (top), Galileo Ramos, 30 (top), gn8 (rays and lines), cover and throughout, GoodFocused, 5 (bottom left and middle), Gulliver20, 14, Guppic the duck, cover (glasses, hat, crown), Hadrani Hasan, 58 (bottom), Happy Together, 17 (top), ishraqahmed, 39 (tortoises in the rocket), James Tysz, 12, Ken Griffiths, 7 (middle), Ketpachara Yoosuk, 60 (bottom), Kurit afshen, 4 (right), 18, Laura Brind Cayman, 32, Lauren Suryanata, 39 (middle), 51 (top), Level2Photographer, 56 (top), Linda McKenna, 58 (top), Maqdis Studio, 52 (top), Mark_Kostich, 5 (top), Matt Jeppson, 61 (top), Michael Rosskothen, 38, moj0j0, 37 (top), Net Vector (waves), 33, 35, NickEvansKZN, 57, Noppe Herlinde, 20 (middle), PetlinDmitry, back cover, 1 (top), 4 (middle), Pranesh Luckan, 34, reptiles4all, 11, 13, 50, Rich Carey, 26 (middle left), 29 (bottom), Richard Whitcombe, 29 (top), Rizvisual, 43 (bottom), Rosa Jay, 6, Samakai, cover (bottom left), schankz, 40 (bottom), somdul, cover (bottom right), Stephen Barnes, 42, Stu Porter, 43 (top), Susan Flashman, 56 (middle), Svetlana Foote, 27, Tawat Hantrakool, 26 (top), TigerStocks, 10, Toxa2x2, 41 (bubbles), v_kulieva (gradient background), back cover and throughout, Valery Evlakhov, 21 (box with bananas), Viktor Thaut, 4 (left), vkilikov, 36 (bottom), WeDevlops, 35 (turtle on the field), Yudi S, 62, ZipDesign, 20 (bottom)

Printed in the United States 6739

TABLE OF CONTENTS

A REPTILIAN FACT COLLECTION!

Did you know that a group of turtles is called a bale, a group of crocodiles is called a bask, and a group of amazing reptile facts is called a **FACT FRENZY**? Get ready to discover all the slithery, scaly, and surprising facts you can—in tiny bites or swallowed whole, like a python does. You'll learn amazing tricks and traits of some of the 11,500 reptiles in our world.

WATCH OUT FOR SHOOTING BLOOD AND VENOMOUS FANGS . . .

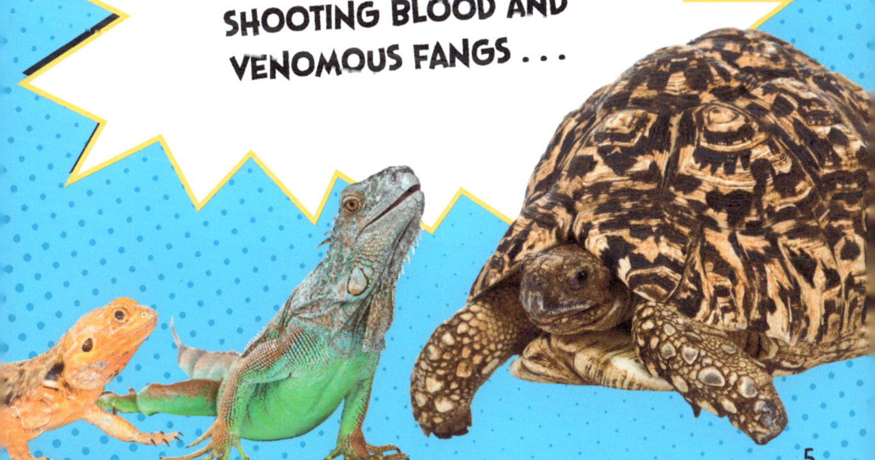

SURPRISING SNAKES

There are more than 3,000 known species of snakes.

The smallest kind of snake would fit inside the mouth of the largest kind.

Some kinds of snakes lay just one egg. Others lay up to 100!

Snakes smell the world around them about once every second when they're chasing prey.

A snake's forked tongue gives it a 3-D "view" of the smells around it.

Snakes do not have ears. They "hear" by feeling vibrations in the ground.

Snakes can have up to 400 vertebrae. Humans have just 33.

The ancestors of modern snakes had legs. Tiny, useless leg bones can still be seen in some snake species.

WOW!

SOME SNAKES ARE BORN WITH TWO HEADS.

A snake's fangs are curved backward. When prey tries to pull back after being bitten, the fangs just dig in deeper.

Snakes lose teeth but constantly grow new ones.

Vipers can fold away their fangs until needed.

The Gaboon viper has the longest fangs of any snake—up to 2 inches (5 centimeters) long!

A Burmese python stretches its jaws to swallow huge prey.

WOW!

THE AFRICAN ROCK PYTHON EATS ANTELOPES AND CROCODILES! IT SUFFOCATES THEM AND SWALLOWS THEM WHOLE.

The green tree python hunts by dangling its tail as bait from a tree branch.

There are 38 different species of cobras. They live in warm places like parts of Asia.

Some spitting cobras can launch their venom more than 10 feet (3 meters).

Scientists study king cobra venom to make medicines.

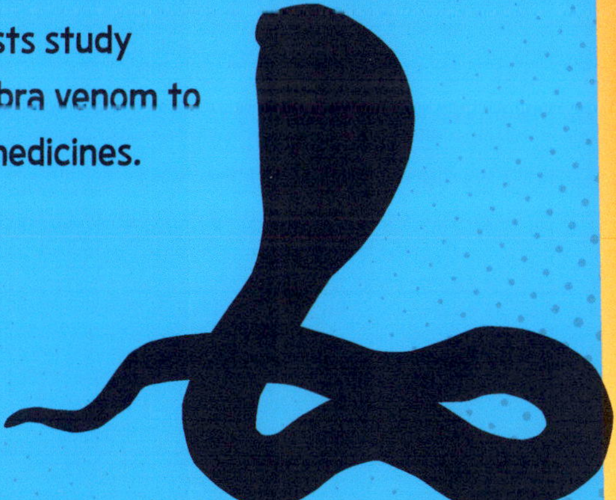

Pit vipers sense body heat using "pit organs" between their eyes and nostrils.

Some snakes can detect temperature changes of just 0.002°F (0.001°C). This helps them find prey in darkness.

WOW!

SCIENTISTS BLINDFOLDED A PIT VIPER, AND IT WAS STILL ABLE TO CATCH ITS PREY.

The eyelash palm pit viper lives in Central America. It has scales above each eye that look like eyelashes.

WOW!

THIS VIPER OFTEN HIDES IN BANANA PLANTS. MANY HAVE ACCIDENTALLY BEEN SENT ALL OVER THE WORLD INSIDE BANANA SHIPMENTS!

The paradise flying snake glides through forests. It jumps from trees and flattens its body like a parachute.

Desert sidewinder snakes throw their bodies in loops across the hot sand to zip along dunes.

Rattlesnakes can swim and have been found in the ocean several miles from shore.

Markings on the Indian cobra look like large eyes. This tricks predators into thinking the snake is larger than it really is.

Puff adders and cobras inflate the front of their bodies to appear larger when threatened.

Up to 40 percent of the liquid in a garter snake's body can freeze and the snake will still survive.

TURTLE AND TORTOISE TRUTHS

There are 328 known species of turtles and tortoises.

WOW!

SOME TORTOISES CAN LIVE TO BE MORE THAN 150 YEARS OLD.

The earliest known turtles lived 220 million years ago.

Tortoises live only on land. Turtles can live on land or in water.

An adult sea turtle can sleep underwater for six hours without going up for air!

Sea turtles "cry" to get rid of extra salt in their bodies.

A turtle's shell is made up of about 50 bones.

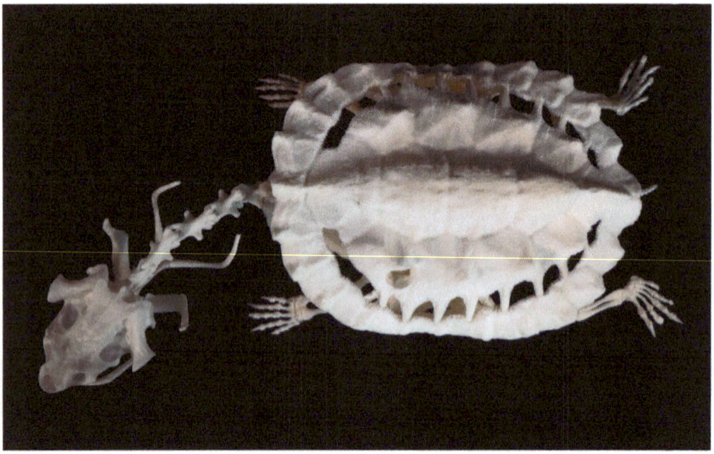

A turtle makes room to hide in its shell by blowing air out of its lungs.

Male turtles hatch from eggs kept at low temperatures. Female turtles hatch from eggs kept at high temperatures.

Turtles have no teeth. Their jaws have sharp edges used to tear meat or plants.

In the 1800s, there was a rumor that a Mexican giant musk turtle had chewed its way out of an alligator's stomach! Scientists today say this is impossible.

The musk turtle is known as the stinkpot turtle. It gives off terrible odors to scare away predators.

A thirsty desert tortoise can drink more than 40 percent of its weight in water. For a 100-pound (45-kilogram) person, that's like drinking 5 gallons (18.9 liters) of water!

In Arizona, the desert box turtle sometimes beats the heat by burrowing into fresh cow poop.

Box turtles often spend their entire lives in an area about the size of a football field.

Young green sea turtles eat both plants and meat, such as jellyfish.

They become herbivores and eat only plants when they reach 10 pounds (4.5 kg) in weight.

Leatherback sea turtles can eat dozens of jellyfish in a single meal.

The Berlandier's tortoise eats the droppings of other tortoises.

WOW!

AN ANCIENT SEA TURTLE CALLED ARCHELON COULD GROW TO BE 12 FEET (3.7 M) LONG!

In ancient China, the patterns on tortoise shells were believed to predict the future.

The Soviet Union launched two tortoises into space in 1968.

The alligator snapping turtle has a wormlike "lure" on the tip of its tongue, which it uses to catch fish.

The North American wood turtle stomps its feet to bring earthworms to the surface. Then it eats them!

WOW!

THE LEATHERBACK SEA TURTLE SOMETIMES MAKES A NOISE THAT SOUNDS LIKE A HUMAN BURP.

INCREDIBLE CROCS AND GATORS

Crocodiles are the biggest and heaviest reptiles on Earth.

The Nile crocodile can reach 20 feet (6 m) long. It can weigh up to 2,000 pounds (900 kg).

Crocodiles bite with a force of up to 5,000 pounds per square inch (350 kg per square cm). Human bites are a wimpy 162 pounds per square inch (11.4 kg per square cm).

American alligators were brought back from the brink of extinction.

There are an estimated 1.3 million alligators in Florida.

Alligators grow new teeth as old ones wear out. One alligator may go through as many as 3,000 teeth in a lifetime!

Alligator and crocodile mothers let their babies swim into their mouths for protection and to carry them.

The slender-snouted crocodile in West Africa can climb trees!

The Cuban crocodile hunts birds. It uses its tail to launch itself into the air from underwater.

LIZARD WIZARDS

Australia's deserts have the most lizard varieties. In some places, up to 40 species live in the same area.

The nano-chameleon is the smallest reptile. It could sit on the tip of your fingernail!

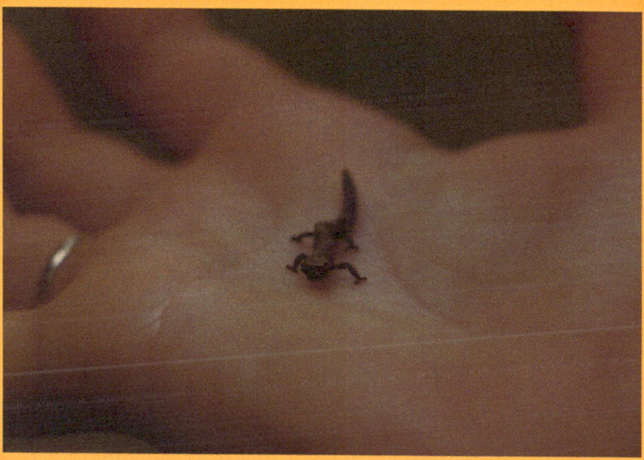

Some lizards can run on their hind legs.

Some lizards, such as the monkey-tailed skink from the Solomon Islands, have green blood.

The coast horned lizard of California sprays predators with blood from its eyes.

On average, a chameleon's tongue is about twice the length of its body!

A chameleon can move its two eyes separately. It can see two different views at once.

The Draco lizard has wide flaps of skin. These flaps allow it to glide from tree to tree.

Fringe-toed lizards "swim" in the desert sand to escape predators.

The green basilisk lizard has long, wide toes that allow it to dash across water for about 15 feet (4.6 m).

Gila monsters spend most of their time underground.

They mainly eat eggs that they steal from birds' nests.

Gila monsters store body fat in their tails. When food is scarce, they can survive on this fat for months without eating.

A shingleback skink's brown scales make it look like a pinecone.

Its tail also looks like its head. It curls into a C shape to confuse predators.

The armadillo lizard curls into a ball and puts its tail into its mouth to protect itself.

Male anole lizards expand their throats when they see a threat.

A frilled lizard opens its neck flaps like an umbrella to scare away predators.

Thorny devil lizards have spikes on their bodies that make them difficult for predators to swallow.

Geckos are noisy! They chirp, click, squeak, and growl.

They have sticky hairs on their feet that allow them to walk on walls or even ceilings.

Geckos shed their tails when threatened. This distracts the predator so the lizard can escape.

Many lizards that lose their tails can regrow them.

A Komodo dragon can eat up to 80 percent of its body weight in just one meal. It can eat 5.5 pounds (2.5 kg) of meat in just one minute!

Adult Komodo dragons sometimes eat baby Komodo dragons.

WOW!

BABY KOMODO DRAGONS ROLL AROUND IN THE GUTS OF DEAD ANIMALS TO HIDE THEIR SCENT FROM HUNGRY ADULTS!

BOOKS IN THIS SERIES

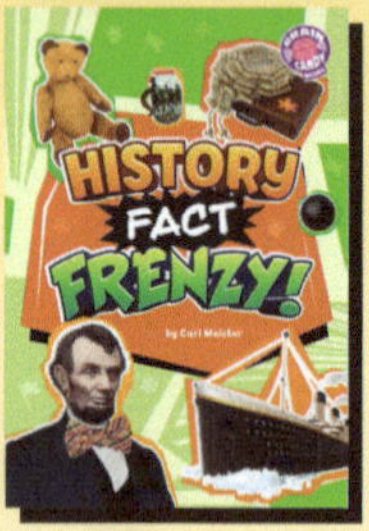

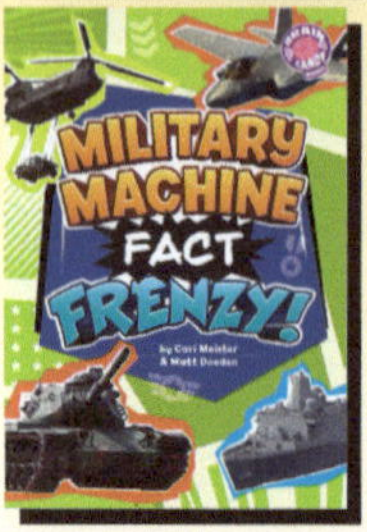